The Miracle in a
Mother's
Hug

The Miracle in a
Mother's
Hug

Helen Burns

 HOWARD BOOKS
A DIVISION OF SIMON & SCHUSTER

New York London Toronto Sidney

OUR PURPOSE AT HOWARD BOOKS IS TO:

- *Increase faith* in the hearts of growing Christians
- *Inspire holiness* in the lives of believers
- *Instill hope* in the hearts of struggling people everywhere

  BECAUSE HE'S COMING AGAIN!

Published by Howard Books, a division of Simon & Schuster
1230 Avenue of the Americas, New York, NY 10020

The Miracle in a Mother's Hug © 2005 by Helen Burns

Library of Congress Cataloging-in-Publication Data
Burns, Helen, 1955–
    The miracle in a mother's hug / Helen Burns.
        p. cm.
    Includes bibliographical references (p.).
    ISBN 978-1-4767-3815-4
    1. Mothers. 2. Mother and child. 3. Love, Maternal. 4. Motherhood. 5. Spiritual life. I. Title.

HQ759.B78 2005
306.874'3—dc22

                                                2004042365

15 14 13 12 11 10 9 8 7 6

HOWARD is a registered trademark of Simon & Schuster, Inc.

Manufactured in the United States of America

For information regarding special discounts for bulk purchases, please contact Simon & Schuster Special Sales at 1-800-456-6798 or business@simonandschuster.com

Edited by Michele Buckingham
Interior design by John Mark Luke Designs

To my daughters,

Angela, Danica, and Ashley.

Heaven smiled on me the day each of you was born.

It has been pure joy and my richest reward

watching you grow to become the most amazing

wives, mothers, and friends.

I'll love you always and forever.

contents

contents

acknowledgments

I would like to acknowledge the greatest cheerleaders in my life: my parents, Peter and Elsy Balzer, who have loved me as perfectly as humanly possible. Your love, faith, and prayers continue to carry me every day of my life.

To John, my husband and my very best friend, who still makes my heart skip a beat when he walks into the room: thank you for believing in me always, making me laugh every day, loving God and me passionately (in that order), and sharing this most amazing adventure of life with me. I love growing older with you.

To Michele Buckingham, editor extraordinaire: thank you for taking my thoughts and words and putting your creative and thoughtful touch upon every page.

Before you were conceived—I wanted you
Before you were born—I loved you
Before you were here an hour—I would die for you
This is the miracle of life

—MAUREEN HAWKINS

The Miracle
in a Mother's Hug

A few years ago, my husband, John, wrote a little book called *The Miracle in a Daddy's Hug*. The title, he explained, has a twofold meaning.

"First, a child being held in a daddy's arms is a unique and wonderful miracle of God's creation," he wrote, "and not just a miracle, but a miracle full of miracles still to be realized. So much life, so much potential is still ahead! Second, a daddy's embrace has miracle-working power. When a father wraps his arms, his words, his love, and his faith around his son or daughter, he opens the way for a miracle in both their lives."[1]

How true! I have seen the miracles with my own eyes—the God-given miracles that are our three beautiful daughters,

Angela, Danica, and Ashley, now fully grown with families of their own; and the specific-instance miracles that have taken place in each of their lives because their daddy consistently showered them with affection, admiration, and love.

I'm so thankful for the miracle in a daddy's hug. As a mother, however, I think it's important to point out that dads don't have a monopoly on miracles. There's a miracle in a mother's hug too!

Amazing Fruit

After twenty-nine years of motherhood, I know. I've seen miracle after miracle take place as my mother's heart has reached out to embrace my daughters in happy times and sad times, easy times and difficult times.

How well I remember the day John and I left Vancouver Grace Hospital in our dilapidated old Austin Mini, carrying home our first newborn, Angela Sunshine. As I held Angela in my arms, I felt absolutely overwhelmed. This child was entirely dependent upon me. I was responsible for feeding, clothing, and caring for her. I was responsible for her very life! And in that moment, I gave my heart away forever. There was no going back. I held little Angela, then Danica, then Ashley, in my close embrace, and the transfer was made. And it was made over and over again throughout their lives, whenever I held them and hugged them and told them I loved them.

Now I have reached the most gratifying stage of my life. I call it my "reward stage." Proverbs 31:31 NKJV says, "Give her of the fruit of her hands, and let her own works praise her in the gates." Now I fully understand the *why* behind the *what* of everything we do as mothers. The future is literally in our hands. Everything that leaves our lives enters our futures. With the wisdom of hindsight, I now know that every bedtime story I read, every prayer I prayed, every tear I kissed away, every encouraging word I spoke, every promise I kept, every memory I made mattered. Every act of love, however insignificant it seemed at the time, left an indelible imprint upon my children's impressionable hearts. I now see the effect of all those hugs given over all those years. I watch in wonder as my daughters now do for their children some of the very same things I did for them when they were young.

It is the most amazing thing to watch those whom you have mothered become mothers and carry forth a legacy you helped create! That wonderful fruit is our reward. But it comes later in life. When we're young mothers, we can't see it; we wonder if there will ever be a return on our unconditional investment in our children's lives. I know I often worried about whether I was doing a good job as a mom. *Am I doing the right thing?* I would ask myself. *Am I getting it right more often than I am messing up? Am I making a difference at all? Does anyone appreciate or even notice that I have changed ten diapers today and done four loads of laundry and made three edible meals and managed to hold it all together until bedtime?* I had this gnawing fear that if my kids messed up, it would be because of me. Every mother, I think, has this fear to some degree.

Thankfully, on the journey of motherhood, I did at least one thing right: I hugged my girls. I showed them lots of affection. I loved them, encouraged them, mentored them, befriended them. And in the process, I discovered the mercy and grace of God. I was not a perfect mother—not even close. None of us is. But God was faithful in every situation, even when I failed. He assured me that as I invested everything I had of my own natural ability, he would add his "super" to my "natural." And the results have been just that: supernatural!

Yes, I went through trying times with my children. Sometimes I thought I wouldn't make it—or that they wouldn't. But because quitting was not a viable option, I kept on venturing ahead with a heart full of hope and faith. I kept on loving. I kept on hugging. And to my amazement, God did miracles.

Miracle Soil

*L*ike a daddy's hug, a mother's hug is made up of several components. The first is the child or, as John says, "that miracle full of miracles in seed form."[2] The second is the mother, who has the God-given responsibility and privilege to nurture and care for her miracle seed. Then there are the nutrients within her "soil" that are necessary for the seed's healthy growth: her touch, her presence, her encouragement, her influence, her commitment, her example, her faith, and her friendship.

As we take a closer look at each of these nutrients in the chapters that follow, my prayer is that this book will produce miracles. May each of us discover in a fresh way the paramount significance of a mother's role in the lives of her children. And may we be encouraged and inspired to be better mothers in the process!

Hold tenderly that which you cherish.

—BOB ALBERTI

The Miracle in a Mother's Touch

To me a word that is synonymous with motherhood is *nurture*. I believe the very essence of motherhood involves nurturing, nourishing, cherishing, treasuring, and supporting our children. And one of the primary ways we do this is through the miracle of touch.

There are few sights more beautiful than that of a mother holding her child, nursing a tiny newborn at her breast, tucking a six-year-old into bed at night, or wrapping her arms around an eighteen-year-old whose heart has been broken for the first time. In these situations and so many others, nothing can take the place of a mother's tender and loving touch.

The Need for Touch

*N*ever underestimate the power of touch. Every child is born with a deep need to be tenderly held and touched in a meaningful way. Study after study has shown that children who are deprived of wholesome touch are more prone to sickness and death than children who are hugged and cuddled often. The research proves what we already know intuitively: there is healing and health in the warmth and security of a loving touch, a hug, a cuddle, a kiss, a pat on the back, or even a high-five.

To be touched in a healthy manner is one of the most fundamental needs known to mankind, yet much of our society bristles at the thought of physical touch because of the negative impressions that have been associated with it. As a pastor, I am very aware of the damage that has been inflicted upon many, many victims of unwholesome touch. Nevertheless, I think it's tragic that what God created for the purpose of helping us grow into healthy men and women has been twisted and undermined to the point that many of us are intimidated and distrustful of all manner of touching.

Wholesome touch and affection are crucial to the well-being of healthy children and strong families. How sad that it is unfamiliar territory for so many of us! Often the problem is the culture in which we were raised. In some cultures, affection is frowned upon and considered unnecessary. Other times, the problem is the home

There is healing and health in the warmth and security of a loving touch.

in which we grew up. If we weren't kissed and cuddled often as children, we may feel uncomfortable displaying affection toward our own kids.

We can't use our backgrounds as an excuse, however. Since God created us with a need for touch, it's imperative that we push through the barriers of culture and upbringing and reach out and touch somebody! Our children were formed with the vital need to be comforted by our touch. They need the physical reassurance that says, "I love you, and I am here for you." We must not back away.

Touch can happen in many meaningful ways. I remember so many scenes from my years of motherhood: the girls and me cuddling under a huge comforter in front of the fireplace after the power went out in our home, massive pileups on top of Daddy when he came in the door, tickle fights, joining hands to say thanks for our food, and holding hands on long walks through the forest. As a family, we were and are completely comfortable with touch, because it has always been pure, healthy, and wholesome.

Just last night, at our weekly Burns family dinner, my granddaughter Madison came to me as I was sitting on the couch. She was carrying a bottle of lotion, and she proceeded to stretch herself across my lap and pull up the back of her shirt. I knew exactly what she wanted: a "shubby." (Most people call it a backrub.) She comes to me for shubbies often, and I hope she doesn't stop. My girls loved getting a comforting backrub from my mother when they were young, and they still do!

Jesus, Our Model

When it comes to tender, wholesome touch, we have no better model than Jesus. Mark 10:13–16 gives us a moving picture:

One day some parents brought their children to Jesus so he could touch them and bless them, but the disciples told them not to bother him. But, when Jesus saw what was happening, he was very displeased with his disciples. He said to them, "Let the children come to me. Don't stop them! For the Kingdom of God belongs to such as these.". . . Then he took the children into his arms and placed his hands on their heads and blessed them.

How beautiful! Surely in that display of affection, those children understood beyond a shadow of a doubt that they were deeply loved by God.

I am also moved by another story about Jesus and touch. In Matthew 8:1–4, a leper came to worship Jesus. Rather than back away from the leper, as most people would have done, Jesus reached out and touched him. And according to verse 3, "instantly the leprosy disappeared." I'm sure that the leper was not only in great need of healing, he was also in need of the simple physical touch of another human being. I wonder how long it had been since he'd felt the warmth of human contact.

As Jesus knew, touch says, "You matter to me right now." It

creates a supernatural sense of closeness and belonging that every person instinctively longs for. We need to be like Jesus and never miss an opportunity to reach out and touch somebody with tenderness—especially our kids!

A beautiful thing happened one Sunday morning in our children's church program. Even now it stands out to me as a powerful example of the need every child has for wholesome affection. A young boy of about five years of age was a consistent challenge to our children's ministry. He often disrupted the class and caused his teacher a lot of frustration. On this particular Sunday, as the teacher was attempting to read the class a story, this young boy once again began behaving in his usual, unruly way. Not knowing what else to do, the teacher told him to come up front and sit on his lap, in hopes that he could keep the boy contained long enough to finish reading the story. To the teacher's great surprise, this little guy cuddled right up to him, burrowed himself into a cozy position, and sat as still as could be. Apparently, the boy was literally starved for human touch. Once he received it, his entire personality changed in an instant.

Truly, touch is miraculous. It has incredible power. In a single moment, it can help and heal; it can call forth calm and reassurance; it can instill courage and confidence. For children in particular, wholesome touch is critical for health and happiness—a necessity, like food and air.

As mothers, it's our job to make sure our kids get all the healthy touch they need. It's our job to hug! There is a miracle in a mother's touch. Let's reach out and make miracles.

Write these commandments that
I've given you today on your hearts.
Get them inside of you and then
get them inside your children.
Talk about them wherever you are,
sitting at home or walking in the street;
talk about them from the time
you get up in the morning
to when you fall into bed at night.

—Deuteronomy 6:6–7 MSG

The Miracle in a Mother's Presence

Inherent in a mother's hug is something so obvious you could almost miss it: her presence. A mother must physically be there for her children in order to nurture them. In fact, children crave their mother's physical presence in their lives. It's paramount to their development. Other people can be important, but there is no replacement for Mom.

The miraculous bond between a mother and child is like no other. It's not just an emotional and spiritual connection; it's also physical. That means that as mothers, we have the ability to convey messages through our words, our actions, and our very presence. Our children take their cues from us. Every time they wake up from a nap or run through the door after school or fall down and hurt themselves, they look to us for comfort, affirmation, and a sense of well-being. *If Mom is there*, they think, *then everything is going to be all right.*

When my children were small, I discovered that they needed me in very practical and real ways: to feed them, dress them, tuck them in at night, and hold their hands when they walked across a busy street. My being there was crucial to virtually every aspect of their daily lives. When they became teenagers, my role changed; but I found that they still wanted me to be there so they could talk to me when life got difficult and they had big (or sometimes even little) decisions to make. Today they still look to me to "be there" for them, albeit in different ways since they are grown and have families of their own.

And that has been my goal: to have my daughters feel that they can come to me at any time for anything. I want them to know beyond a shadow of a doubt that whatever their age, wherever they are in the world, I would do almost anything to be with them when they say, "I need you, Mom."

A child doesn't pick up that understanding by accident; it is communicated by design. As moms, we need to build a confidence in our children that says, "You are important to me, and your feelings and thoughts are safe with me." We get that message across most clearly when we make ourselves emotionally and physically available to our kids. Just being there for your children speaks volumes!

T·I·M·E

One of the greatest privileges my daughters (and sons-in-law) have shared with me in recent years has been the opportunity to be present with them during the births of my grandchildren, Madison, Miller, and Medo. What deep satisfaction, wonder, and awe I felt as I watched the beautiful transmission of nurture being passed from generation to generation in those moments! As the newborns were placed into their mothers' arms—recipients of their very first hug—I could almost literally see the love and care that began to flow freely from mother to child.

Those moments convinced me more than ever that mothers have an innate ability to nurture their children. Unfortunately, that ability is often short-circuited when moms, for whatever reason, make themselves inaccessible.

For a child, love is spelled T-I-M-E. Sadly, many mothers mistakenly assume that they can give their children *quality* time without investing a *quantity* of time. I have learned, however, that you can't develop quality time with kids without spending lots of quantity time with them. Too much love or time spent with children will never spoil them! Children become spoiled when parents substitute *presents* for *presence*. Our children need us, not things—and that means we must make an investment of time.

Time together as a family was always very important in our home. Recently I asked my daughters to tell me some of their favorite childhood memories. To my surprise, the simplest things meant the most to them—things like riding our bikes together through the neighborhood (we all took on code names of well-known bike racers, since John was a cycling fan); walking through the forest picking bouquets of wildflowers; the "big event" of getting haircuts and sporting the

You can't develop quality time with kids without spending lots of quantity time with them.

latest 'do; a trip to Woodward's candy store to buy a dollar's worth of sours; making "teddy bear" bread on rainy days (we formed the dough into a teddy bear shape, with raisins for the eyes, nose, and mouth); family nights at the swimming pool; singing silly songs in the backseat of the car; making a big deal of getting ready for Daddy before he came home for dinner; staging fashion shows and plays in the backyard; going on school field trips (Ashley told me, "You were the best mom, because you took our carload to Mac's Market for Slurpees"); bath times in the big brown tub; going for ice cream with our friends the Carlsons after church on Sunday nights—the list could go on and on. The common denominator? We were together. We were spending quality time *and* quantity time.

Together on Purpose

Few truly magnificent things happen by accident; truly significant things happen on purpose. When my children were growing up, I often pulled out my best dishes and set a beautiful, candlelit table for dinner. When the girls would come home after school and see the table so elaborately set, they would get excited and ask, "Who is coming for dinner?" I delighted in answering, "You are!" and seeing the beautiful smiles on their faces. They understood from that simple act that they were the really special guests in my life and that I loved being with them.

In our home, we had a number of traditions that helped nurture our togetherness. One of these was our weekly family night, which always involved the five of us doing something fun together. Whether we went swimming, bowling, or out to the movies, our entire goal for the evening was to laugh a lot and enjoy one another.

When the girls started reaching adulthood and getting married, however, the family-night tradition gradually got left behind. After all, they had families of their own now. And besides, John and I were busier than ever, ministering more and more frequently away from home and around the world.

But family night was never forgotten. In fact, my daughters eventually let me know that they missed me and the connection we always made during those regular family times. Danica expressed it this way: "As grownups and wives, we were missing you as you traveled the world. We just wanted your friendship— to have you around to see that we were doing well, to be proud of us and interested in our lives. That desire never goes away. It just evolves." I choke up as I write this, because I feel so blessed that my children want me in their lives at every level even still. So now, on a typical Monday night, you will find John and me, our daughters and sons-in-law, and our grandchildren gathered at our home for the Burns family night. And if John and I happen to be out of town, the rest of the family will be there anyway!

Seize the Moment

Now that I am a grandmother, I think I'm becoming a lot like my mom. When John and I were young parents, we lived for six years in a town that was 350 miles north of my parents' home in Vancouver. My parents were desperately lonely for their grandchildren during that period. I remember my father calling me several days after one of our visits to their house, informing me that my mother had left the girls' fingerprints on her kitchen window. Rather than wash them off, she would outline each one of them with her finger and try to guess which fingerprint belonged to which granddaughter: Angela, Danica, or Ashley.

At the time, the thought of fingerprints anywhere made me nervous. (I was a little obsessive about cleanliness in the early days). I couldn't imagine why Mom would leave the marks on her window for so long. But I understand completely now, and I tend to follow her example with my own grandchildren. Messes can always be cleaned up later, but children grow up all too quickly. Time waits for no one. As mothers (and grandmothers!), we must seize each precious moment and make the very most of it.

After all, people lying on their deathbeds never wish they had spent more time at the office. But many regret that they didn't spend more time with their family and friends.

The lyrics to the Harry Chapin song "Cat's in the Cradle" have always gripped my heart:

And the cat's in the cradle and the silver spoon,
Little boy blue and the man in the moon.
"When you coming home, son?"
"I don't know when, but we'll get together then, Dad.
You know we'll have a good time then."[1]

The song tells the sad, but all-too-typical, story of a dad who never had time for his son during his parenting years, only to discover that later, when he's retired and has lots of time on his hands, his now-grown, very busy son doesn't have time for *him*. Unfortunately, the same story can be told of many mothers.

Life is made up of moments—moments that present us with opportunities to love, nurture, care, and hug. We need to grasp these moments while we can, because we can never get them back again. If we don't seize the opportunities we have today to spend time with our children, we effectively give up our rights to a wonderful future with them later in life.

The Next Chapter

Of all the many hugs I have shared with my children through the years, one in particular has been indelibly printed upon my heart. It happened the night before Angela, my oldest, was to be married—the first of three weddings that I would plan and prepare for my daughters. We had finished all the preparations and were completely exhausted, but I stayed up and waited for an opportunity to connect with Angela before we went to bed that night.

When she walked into the living room, I invited her to sit with me on the couch for a moment. We didn't have to speak any words; our hearts understood what words could not express. Being together was enough.

"I knew I had my mom on my team, cheering me on."

As I hugged her and held her close, she began to cry as if her heart would break. I understood: her life would never be the same again. She was feeling a "tearing" in her heart—not a painful or damaging tear, but one that was releasing her to begin the brand-new life that she had dreamed of from the time she was a little girl.

Finally, after hugging her for a long time, I took Angela's face in my hands and wiped her tears.

"Angela," I told her, "this is not the end of the book—just the end of a chapter in a beautiful book that is *your* life. Tomorrow you will begin to write upon a brand-new page, and many more chapters will be written in the days ahead."

Angela later told me her perspective about that moment: "As lost as I felt at the prospect of leaving the nest and growing into my new role as a wife, I also felt overwhelmed with gratitude. I knew I had my mom on my team, cheering me on."

It didn't matter that Angela was an adult woman about to start a new life and a new family. She needed her mom to be there for her that night. And I want to be there still, for her and for each of my children and grandchildren.

As mothers, let's commit ourselves to being actively present in our children's lives. Our roles may have to adapt as each new chapter is written, but the end result is sure to be a story full of miracles.

My mother said to me,
"If you become a soldier, you'll be a general;
if you become a monk, you'll end up as the pope."
Instead, I became a painter and wound up as Picasso.

—PABLO PICASSO

The Miracle in a Mother's Encouragement

*E*verybody needs a cheerleader, and there's no cheerleader like a mother. How many times have you seen huge athletes in the National Football League (some as big as refrigerators!) running toward the field to play a big game? As soon as they notice the TV cameras, they turn into little boys, smiling, waving, and calling out, "Hi, Mom!" They were born wanting their mommies to be there for them. And even after they are grown men, they still need Mom to be their number one fan. I think that's awesome!

I am forever grateful to my own mom, who has been the greatest encourager in my life. I can't remember a single moment in my life when she didn't make me feel supported and loved. I know I owe a lot to her. When I think of Mom, I think of being treasured, cherished, and valued. I think of the way her face always lit up with delight whenever I walked into the room. I think of the hugs she gave that let me know I was deeply loved. It is from my mother that I learned the value of celebrating each of my own children as individuals and encouraging them to be the best God made them to be.

My three children were born within a period of three and a half years. Yes, I was busy! But even though all three are girls and very close in age, I realized early on that they needed to be treated as individuals with very specific needs and desires. They needed me to connect one-on-one with them and give them the special, individual attention they craved. They needed to know how glad I was that out of all the mothers in the world God could have chosen for them, he allowed me the honor and privilege of being their mom.

The fact is, all children need a mother's encouragement. Their self-esteem is derived largely from Mom's acceptance and love toward them from infancy on. This means throughout the parenting years, our hugs have to speak volumes, and so do our words. Every word we say—good and bad, positive and negative—is woven into their character, which ultimately is woven into the fabric of society. The family unit, like no other institution in the world, must be the one place where unconditional love and encouragement is freely given and spoken!

Rules for Moms

When it comes to encouragement, there are four rules moms need to live by:

1. Never miss an opportunity to tell your children how much you love them.

We may assume that our sons and daughters know that we love them. And hopefully, they do. Still, we should never miss an opportunity to tell them how valuable they are to us.

In fact, our entire being should demonstrate our love and approval of our children. According to communication experts, our words make up a mere 7 percent of the message we convey; the other 93 percent comes from our body language and tone of voice. As we speak with our kids, they need to be able to look into our eyes and see how we feel about them. (After all, the eyes are the window to the soul and express what is deepest within us. Children know this intuitively.) Our sons and daughters must be able to feel our love through tender pats, touches, and hugs.

September 11, 2001, is a day that indelibly imprinted this principle on my heart. Along with the rest of the world, I watched the tragedy of planes crashing and buildings crumbling in those early morning hours. As I sat glued to the television, two little angels—my grandchildren, Madison and Miller—walked into the room with dreamy, sleepy faces, one dragging her "blankie" and the other pulling a teddy bear behind him. I held both of them close and kissed their sweet faces over and over again. I was so aware of the significance of the moment. I remember thinking, *The thousands of people who died today will never have another opportunity to tell their loved ones "I love you"—at least not in this lifetime.*

"I will always love you."
"I will love you forever."

"Oma loves you very much," I said to my grandchildren, hugging them tightly. They'd heard it many times before, but I wanted to say it again. "You are my favorite treasures in the world!"

That morning I was reminded: treat every day as a gift, because it may be your last. Since September 11, I have tried to make it a priority to express my love and affection to the special people in my life. I've felt compelled to choose my words wisely—to only say things that will bring a blessing to those who hear them.

2. Be sure to speak the words always and forever.

As moms, we need to declare our unconditional love and commitment to our children—a love and commitment they can count on for the rest of their lives. We need to say things such as, "I will *always* love you," "I will love you *forever*," and "Nothing you could ever do would make me love you less, and nothing you could ever do would make me love you more." These kinds of statements speak volumes to our children. They build confidence, security, and self-worth deep into their souls.

3. *Practice the ten-to-one rule.*

Whenever I speak to women's groups, I encourage mothers to follow the ten-to-one rule with their kids: for every one word of correction you speak, be sure to speak ten words of encouragement. This is more difficult than it sounds. As mothers, we often fall into the habit of nagging in order to get our children to do the things we want them to do. But the fact is, nagging will never produce the positive results that encouragement and appropriate discipline will.

Hindsight can be a wonderful teaching tool, so allow me to share a lesson I learned the hard way. Recently Angela reminded me of how much I used to nag her about her messy closet when she was a teenager. Poor child—she endured so much ranting and raving from me! In almost every respect, Angela was the poster child for perfect kids. The rest of her room was kept reasonably clean; only the closet was a mess. But I allowed that closet to drive me to distraction! If I could relive those days, you know what I would do? I would shut up and shut the door. I would choose a more important battle to fight. I wouldn't allow so many words to go toward the negative pattern of nagging.

4. Let your words be the words that speak the loudest to your children's hearts.

So many voices speak into our children's lives. And sadly, so many of those voices—whether at school, in the community, or through the media—are negative and potentially damaging. As moms, we need to make sure that *our* words are the ones that are laying a healthy foundation in our children's hearts.

During the formative years of our daughters' lives, John and I had a little ritual that we practiced on a daily basis. At breakfast we would pray a blessing over our food and then a blessing over our girls. Next we all would recite together a statement that went something like this: "Thank you, God, that I am wonderfully created; I was born to be blessed and to be a blessing. Thank you, God, that you love me; therefore I love others, and others love me. Thank you that everything I do today is blessed by your hand, and I am protected and safe in your loving care."

Through this simple habit and in many other ways, we encouraged our girls to expect to be loved. We taught them that as they loved others, others would love them back. As a result, they developed the expectation that people would think positively of them and be kind and friendly toward them. They learned to believe for the very best!

This positive expectation was reflected in a parent/teacher meeting that John and I attended with Ashley's first-grade teacher, Mrs. Funnell. At first, when Mrs. Funnell told us that she had never met a first-grader quite like Ashley, I got a little nervous. Was that a good or bad thing? But then she went on to explain that Ashley was a remarkable little girl who possessed incredible confidence. "I don't think the thought has ever occurred to Ashley that the whole world doesn't just love her!" she said.

How wonderful is that? The amazing thing is that today, twenty years later, Ashley still has that same endearing quality. Even though she has learned a few of life's lessons the hard way and has experienced some rejection over the years, in the very core of her being, Ashley still lives life as if everyone loves her. Our words and actions of love, encouragement, and approval formed the first layers on the foundation of her heart, and nothing has been able to move her from that rock-solid base.

Overflowing Love

Ultimately it is from the overflow of our hearts that we speak love and encouragement into the lives of our children. But we can't give away what we don't possess. The good news is, even if we never received love and encouragement from our own parents when we were young—if we were never hugged or told, even once, that we were valued and special— we have a Father in heaven who loves us with an eternal, unshakable love. We are so valuable to him that he sent his son, Jesus, to pay the penalty for our sins and pave the way for us to discover the enormity and wonder of his loving approval.

As moms, let's allow this miraculous love to fill our hearts. Let's allow God's Word to encourage us deep inside. Then we can impart to our sons and daughters the love and encouragement that we've received, knowing that we've started a chain reaction of miracles that will bless us, our children, and generations to come.

The mother's heart is the child's schoolroom.

—H. W. BEECHER

The Miracle in a Mother's Influence

What a powerful role God has presented to us as mothers! We have the opportunity to exert tremendous power in the lives of our children—not so much because we're bigger and stronger than they are (for a few years anyway) or because we're the ones with parental authority. Rather, our power comes from the unique position we have to influence our children's lives. Proverbs 22:6 NKJV tells us to "train up a child in the way he should go, and when he is old he will not depart from it." That's *influence*—and influence, not control or authority, is what ultimately has the greatest, most powerful impact on our kids.

I know this to be true in my own life. What I am and who

I have become is due in great part to the influence of my mother. She taught me not so much by the words she spoke but by the influence of her life upon mine. Influence is not absorbed with our minds but with our hearts. That's why hugs and cuddles and other demonstrations of love are so important; they open the door to the heart so that influence can come in. My mother's love opened my heart from an early age, and her influence impacts me to this very day.

Control and authority can move people for a while, but it is the nature of all human beings to be directed more by those who influence them than by those who have authority over them. That means that as moms, we have to do more than exercise authority; we have to develop influence. We have to ask ourselves, who (or what) is influencing our children the most? We live in a generation obsessed by the influence of media, music, movies, and the like. Do these forces have the greatest influence in our children's lives—or do we? Who is leading the way?

The Gift of a Healthy Heart

These questions have been a great motivation for me to live my life in a way that positively influences my children and grandchildren. For example, many years ago, when I was pregnant with my youngest daughter, I found myself in a place of brokenness and despair. Angela was three, Danica was two, and I was at a critical crossroads in my life. My marriage was in crisis, and I had to make a huge decision: whether to leave my marriage or stay and try to work things out.

Everything within me wanted to run. The amount of work it would take to fix my marriage seemed overwhelming. Leaving seemed to be the easiest route out of the pain. I was at the brink of forfeiting all the dreams I'd ever had of being a good wife and mother.

That's when I had a powerful encounter with God. One lonely

> *We have to do more than exercise authority; we have to develop influence.*

night, in total desperation, I cried out to God and found him to be right there, reaching out his hand to help me. I discovered his love and forgiveness; and in that one moment, God touched my life and began to heal and mend my broken heart and shattered dreams. That night I began a new journey with God—a journey that has brought me all the way to the place I am today.

My life did not transform overnight, but day by day I discovered the faithfulness of God. I discovered how much he loved me, and I began to build my life on his promises. I found myself dreaming again. I began flourishing in life. Over time my marriage was restored, and I grew in my confidence as a mother.

One of the greatest gifts we can give our children is the influence of a healthy heart and soul. Proverbs 4:23 tells us, "Above all else, guard your heart, for it affects everything you do." Our hearts can be compared to the engine of our lives: when we take care of it, it will take us safely on our journey. If our hearts aren't healthy, however, our lives won't be healthy, and we'll set up the generations that follow us to be unhealthy too. We are our children's role models, whether we want to be or not. We lead them into their future. By our influence, we determine largely whether they will succeed or fail in life.

How grateful I am that God met me at my point of need and restored a healthy heart within me! As a result, I was able to pass on the gift of a healthy heart to my children.

The Power of a Mother's Choices

I remember looking at Angela through teary eyes on her wedding day. There she stood, in all the splendor of that special moment, holding on to the arm of her daddy, ready to walk down the aisle toward her soon-to-be husband, Rod. She was smiling and radiant; John was stoic, trying his best to hold himself together. As I took in the magnificent picture before me, so many thoughts could have filled my mind; but only one thought captured my attention in that moment: *Thank God I didn't quit.* I knew I was looking at one of those miracles that happen when a mother makes choices that positively influence her children's lives.

There is so much riding on a mother's choices! My daughters, my grandchildren, our church congregation, those I've had the opportunity to teach at home or abroad, our television audience, and so many others have been influenced by my choices. Scripture challenges us to understand the power of our choices and the influence they have upon generations: "Today I have given you the choice between life and death, between blessings and curses. I call on heaven and earth to witness the choice you make. Oh, that you would choose life, that you and your descendants might live!" (Deuteronomy 30:19).

I've been given many beautiful gifts throughout my life, but none more treasured than the letters I've received from each of my daughters on their wedding nights. These letters are my trophies—my prize! The movie industry has Oscars and the music industry has Grammys, but I have my letters, written straight from my daughters' hearts.

After Rod and Angela's wedding, John, Danica, Ashley, and I came home to find letters from Angela propped on each of our pillows. I opened mine and read it with tears pouring down my face. Her words made me realize, yet again, how quickly the moments and years fly by. The beautiful chapter of life with Angela living in our home had closed; a new chapter was being written, and many more wonderful chapters would follow. Allow me to share her letter with you:

Dear Mom,

I want you to know how very, very thankful I am that God gave me a mother like you. How can I even begin to

tell you how much your love—your unconditional love and support—has meant to me? You should have been thanked thousands of times more often than you actually were. I have so many beautiful, wonderful memories of a happy childhood, because you dedicated yourself to help me. Thank you, Mom, for spending time with me, for playing with me and teaching me to learn, for keeping me fed and making me feel like the most special little girl in the world. Thank you for teaching me to be a lady, for disciplining me, and for loving me regardless of how well I did at anything.

Thank you for working on your marriage and being unselfish, so that I could have a wonderful home. I am so grateful. You really are my hero in this life—I just hope that one day when I have children myself, I will bring them up the way you did, so that their lives can point to the greatness of their grandmother. There really isn't anyone like you. I love you so much. And I am going to miss you—I know I'll grow into my new role, but for now, I'll miss you. Thank you for all the work and energy and love you put into my wedding. I don't know how to tell you *how it makes me feel to have someone like you on my team. You are the best mother in the world! That's final!*

All my love,
Angela

Mothers have incredible power in the lives of their children. May we, as mothers, choose to live in a way that leaves a positive imprint on the ones we love most!

Strength and dignity are her
clothing and her position is strong
and secure; she rejoices over the future
[the latter day or time to come,
knowing that she and her family
are in readiness for it]!

—Proverbs 31:25 AMP

The Miracle in a Mother's Commitment

I enjoyed the most incredible start to my day this morning. Before the dawn broke, I got up and made myself a cup of coffee, grabbed my Bible, and began to enjoy a beautiful time alone with God. After a while, my daughter Danica came into the room carrying her two-month-old daughter, Medo. Without a word she handed Medo to me. For a long time, I cuddled with my precious little bundle, gushing over every adorable smile and coo.

As I held and hugged Medo, the most stunning sunrise began to burst forth, lighting up the ocean outside my living-room window. So there I sat—in awe of the splendor of the morning, filled with absolute wonder at the miracle in my arms, thinking, *What blessings God has poured into my life!*

It is at such moments that I'm glad I held on to God in my darkest times. With fresh awareness of my many blessings, I am once again thankful for the stubborn faithfulness and unwavering commitment of God's love and mercy toward me.

I want to demonstrate that same unwavering commitment to Danica, Medo, and all my special loved ones. Commitment, I'm convinced, is one of the most critical components in a mother's hug. It says to a child, "I'm not going anywhere. We're in this together. Your life is safe with me." Our children need to know that we've made a life-long, unconditional commitment to them and that nothing they do will ever change that. They need to know that in the good times and the bad times, we will be there for them. When we're truly committed to our children's well-being, our hugs and other expressions of love communicate strength, stability, and security to their hearts.

Commitment, I'm convinced, is one of the most critical components in a mother's hug.

A Picture of Commitment and Strength

*C*ommitment is so important! Our children are at great risk for trouble and failure in life if we are not strong, confident, and committed women and mothers. I love the thirty-first chapter of Proverbs, which gives us a picture of such a woman. Among others things, the Proverbs 31 woman is clothed in "strength and dignity," "her position is strong and secure," and she's ready for whatever the future brings (v. 25 AMP). In other words, she knows who she is, what she's doing, and where she's going.

I have to admit, for a while I thought this Proverbs 31 "chick" was a real pain. The more I looked at her life, the more dismayed I became with mine. I realized I had a lot of work ahead of me to become like this biblical paragon. Nevertheless, I knew I wanted to pattern myself after her. She is a great example for all women to follow and aspire to. When we do the work necessary to build strong marriages, strong homes, and strong spiritual lives, as the Proverbs 31 woman did, we demonstrate our commitment to our children and hand them a positive legacy that they can carry forward into future generations.

chapter five

Leaving a Lasting Legacy

Over the course of my own life, I've discovered several things that mothers can do to walk out their commitment to their children and leave behind a lasting legacy:

1. Love Dad.

One of the most important things I've done to show my commitment, build security, and deposit a positive vision for the future into my children's lives is to love their father—to demonstrate my love for him through my words, my affection, and my honor and respect toward him. When a husband and wife are close and tender toward each other—when they resist the urge to be cold and indifferent—they prepare the way for their children to dream beautiful dreams for their own futures as wives and husbands.

Of course, none of us is perfect. I certainly was not perfect in showing love toward John when my girls were growing up. What became obvious, however, was that whenever my heart didn't feel close and safe with John's, my children noticed. It made a huge difference in how secure they felt. As moms, we need to commit ourselves to loving our husbands and do our best to follow through.

2. Create a peaceful atmosphere in the home.

In any home, the mother is the one with her finger on the "atmosphere thermometer." We have a special responsibility to maintain our homes in a way that promotes security and peace for ourselves and our family members.

Our homes are a direct reflection of who we are. As a result, the condition of our homes has a significant impact on how we feel about ourselves; and that, in turn, has a significant impact on how others feel when they're around us. Personally, I want my house to be clean and organized, yet with a comfortable, "lived-in" feeling. I want its décor and atmosphere to be infused with a spirit of hospitality, generosity, and excellence.

Chaos creates crisis. If we allow our homes to be undisciplined, disorganized, and chaotic, we set up our families to live in constant crisis mode. We need to commit ourselves to creating homes that reflect our hearts—and to creating hearts that are at peace.

3. Put first things first.

Everyone has priorities. And everyone lives out those priorities, whether they are aware of what they're doing or not. It's not enough to say, "My children are a priority." If we never find (or make) time in our lives to be with our children, we are kidding ourselves. Nor is it enough to say, "My relationship with God is a priority." If we spend more time watching television than reading our Bibles or praying, soap operas are the priority, not God.

We have to face the truth about our current priorities and commit ourselves to the *right* priorities—those that reflect the constant, love-centered values by which God has called us to live. After all, our priorities determine our goals and long-range plans. They shape the direction of our lives and influence the lives of others, especially our children. When we're confident about our top priorities, we are compelled to eliminate the things, people, activities, and distractions that so readily clutter our lives, making it easier to concentrate on what is truly important. And who are the benefactors? Our children. We create beautiful legacies when we consistently give the greatest attention and place the greatest value on the things that matter most.

4. Build family traditions.

Traditions provide each family with a unique legacy. They are a way of life passed on from generation to generation—an unwritten history that gives a family a special way to define itself.

Those who know me well know that my all-time favorite movie is *Fiddler on the Roof.* When I was dating John, I somehow convinced him to go to the theater to see it with me three times. Understand, it's a musical, and it's l-o-n-g. Nothing gets blown up. There are no racecars. It's definitely not a testosterone-driven movie. I am still amazed that John was willing to see it so often, purely for love's sake!

The message in the movie captivated me then, and it continues to do so today. In the opening, the main character, Tevye, a Jewish peasant in pre-revolutionary Russia, speaks these profound words:

A fiddler on the roof? Sounds crazy, no? But in our little village of Anatevka, you may say every one of us is a fiddler on the roof, trying to scratch out a pleasant, simple tune without breaking his neck. It isn't easy, you know. You may ask, "Why do you stay up there if it is so dangerous?" We stay because Anatevka is our home. And how do we keep our balance? That I can tell you in one word: tradition! Because of our traditions, we've kept our balance for many, many years. Because of our traditions, everyone knows who he is and what God expects him to do.[1]

Tevye had it right: family traditions add a beautiful stability to our lives. In a world where everything is always changing, we need at least a few constants—a few things we can count on, no matter what. I am convinced that children who grow up with family traditions have a better chance of becoming resilient adults, because a place of safety and security has already been built into their lives. It's as if a place at the dinner table of life has been set just for them. The underlying message shouts, "You belong here, and it wouldn't be the same without you!" They can feel free to join in the dinner conversation at any time, because the avenues of communication are wide open to them. There is a blissful familiarity that is so delicious!

Few people really understand the power of family traditions, because they see them as bondage rather than a blessing. That misconception results when traditions are enforced out of a sense of duty rather than encouraged out of a heart of love. My parents were outstanding in this regard. After John and I were married, they truly released us to create our own

Family traditions add a beautiful stability to our lives.

traditions and do whatever we felt was best for us and our new family. I never felt pressured to be at every family event or guilty if I missed calling on an anniversary. But because of the freedom my parents gave us, John and I found ourselves *wanting* to be with them often. We *wanted* to be part of their get-togethers and family traditions. (Lesson: give your children wings to fly, and watch how often they fly back home to be where they feel loved, valued, and celebrated!)

Some of the traditions John and I embraced for our own family started more by accident than by design. One of our favorites has become especially dear to us since the girls have gotten married. It happens on Christmas Eve, when we gather at our house after most of the festivities have already taken place. Each of us opens a present that I've picked out, and it's always the same thing: pajamas. All of the sets match—the guys', the girls', the kiddies', even the ones for John and me. Then we all change into our new outfits and take our annual Burns Christmas photo. (Our sons-in-law are really great sports to go along with this!)

Afterward we gather around, fill our glasses with sparkling apple juice, and begin the toasts. This is the crowning, golden moment of my year! As we raise our glasses, we each share from our hearts about the best parts of the previous twelve months, the hardest parts, the things we're most thankful for—and soon the tears begin spilling. What a blessing it is to be in such a safe, supportive environment, where people can be real with one another! Even the grandchildren get in on the toasting and share the loveliest thoughts. I especially love hearing from my gorgeous sons-in-law, who have the biggest hearts on the planet. Each one is very much a "man's man," but each also has enough heart-strength to open up and be vulnerable.

The beauty of this one tradition is that it has spilled over into other days of the year. It's not just a Christmas Eve ritual anymore. Now my grandchildren, Madison and Miller, regularly raise their juice glasses and offer up a toast, even if we're all out on the deck enjoying a summertime barbecue. Life is great!

Hugs That Go On and On

Meaningful traditions, right priorities, peaceful homes, loving relationships: all of these are expressions of our commitment. They are like big, wonderful, ongoing hugs, conveying the life-giving message, "I love you, and I'm committed to you." As mothers, we need to demonstrate our commitment to our children and our families. Not only will we provide a foundation of safety and stability on which our sons and daughters can build their lives; we will create a wonderful legacy that can be carried forward for generations to come.

How do you measure success? To laugh often and much; to win the respect of intelligent people and the affection of children; to win the appreciation of honest critics and endure the betrayal of false friends; to appreciate beauty; to find the best in others; to leave the world a bit better, whether by a healthy child, a redeemed social condition, or a job well done; to know even one other life has breathed because you lived— this is to have succeeded.

—RALPH WALDO EMERSON

The Miracle in a Mother's Example

One of the most significant miracle's in a mother's hug is the miracle of her example. When we hug our sons and daughters and show them lots of healthy physical affection, we set an example that serves them well for the rest of their lives. Children who grow up knowing they are deeply loved are more capable as adults of loving deeply. They know what healthy love looks like and feels like, because they've seen it in their parents' example.

In so many ways, we teach and lead our children by our example. For that reason, it's important to ask ourselves some hard questions: What will become of our children if they follow in our footsteps? If they follow our lead, will they find themselves on a pathway of peace and blessing or of chaos and crisis?

We must not become so self-absorbed, so focused on our own pain and struggles, that we fail to recognize the impact of our example on our kids. I admit that I was guilty of this kind of self-absorption at one point, before I had a significant encounter with God. The truth is, if I hadn't realized the need to make radical changes in my life, I would have left huge mountains of burden for my children to overcome.

We must parent on purpose. In parenting, as in most things in life, extraordinary outcomes require extraordinary effort. We need to do everything we can to help our children develop a repertoire of skills and tools that will ensure their success in future relationships and pursuits. Their growing-up years are their practice time; the family is their preparation field. And we are their examples, their models, and their mentors. Our task is to lead them into the brightest future possible.

A Love of Learning

Of all the life skills I wanted to impart to my children when they were growing up, a love of learning is one that I considered essential. From an early age, each of my girls knew that reading was not an option in our home; it was a necessity. John and I read often, and we made reading time a vital part of our daughters' training. We spent endless hours in delight and wonder, sharing journeys of discovery through the pages of the books we read together.

As mothers, we do our children a great disservice when we permit them to sit for hours in front of a television set rather than insisting on more productive activities that advance their personal training and development. All kids are born with a natural curiosity and a desire to learn. We need to help them use this wonderful gift to their advantage! Hours spent on a piano bench, at a dance studio, in a swimming pool, on a playing field, or reading a book pay much higher dividends than hours spent on a couch watching TV.

In parenting, as in most things in life, extraordinary outcomes require extraordinary effort.

Helping our children develop a love for learning, however,

requires three things from us. The first is discipline. It's so much easier to let things slide with our kids than to discipline ourselves to make sure they learn and grow! The second is time. Personal growth and development always take time—both our children's and our own.

The third requirement is the theme of this chapter: our example. We need to show our children that we, too, find life to be an interesting, exciting adventure, full of discoveries yet to be made. We need to ask ourselves, how much are we learning, growing, and changing? When is the last time we did something for the first time? I have a magnet on my refrigerator that says, "Do something every day that scares you." I try to live by that rule, for my own sake and for the sake of the example I'm setting for my children and grandchildren.

Allow me to add one more point while we're talking about learning. I firmly believe that nothing is more valuable in a child's development than learning the truth of the Word of God. Many parents are willing to spend hours taking their children back and forth to piano lessons and soccer practice, but they can't seem to get their children to church on Sundays or find time to say prayers with them at night. How sad is that?

What kind of example does it set? If we are more willing to commit time to our children's intellectual and physical advancement than to their spiritual lives, we and they will pay a price. When it comes to our children's development, we need to keep a healthy balance between mind, body, and spirit.

The Value of Laughter

*P*roverbs 17:22 NKJV says, "A merry heart does good, like medicine, but a broken spirit dries the bones." Just as a car needs oil to keep the engine running smoothly, we need laughter in our homes to keep our families running smoothly. As moms, we need to set an example in this regard by showing our children how to instantly brighten their lives through laughter. When life becomes routine, dull, and boring—when we begin to take ourselves too seriously—that's the time to do some serious laughing!

One of the most wonderful memories I have of growing up is the sound of laughter in my home. My parents are both notorious pranksters, and they love to laugh. I inherited this quality from them; and as a result, John, the girls, and I have learned not to take ourselves too seriously but rather to enjoy ourselves and each other. Our dinner table is almost always surrounded with laughter. I'm convinced that our ability to laugh together through the years has played a big part in developing the friendship we now share.

The Power of Love and Forgiveness

Recently Danica told me that one of the most important life lessons she learned from me came from those times when I said, "I'm sorry; please forgive me" and then followed through with whatever changes were called for. "It always amazed me whenever you would humble yourself, communicate with me that you were sorry, and then alter how you parented to make things work better for us," she said. "Doing that validated my individual voice and showed respect and kindness. It made me love and respect you that much more in return."

As I read those words again, I'm reminded of what our children need most from us. I like to call it "parenting by heart": giving our children the grace to fail and the strength to get back up again simply by opening our hearts to lead the way. As moms, we need to be willing to be vulnerable, to admit mistakes, to forgive, and to ask forgiveness. Danica and I learned this through many tears and trials. But what a victory we celebrate today, having grown closer through the challenges we faced together!

You see, at the age of thirteen, Danica developed an eating disorder. We understood very little about it at the time, but it became a battle that she would fight for almost ten years. Looking back now, I can truly appreciate what an incredible fighter she was—and is. We learned a lot about ourselves and each other on her journey toward wholeness.

Many days I wanted to crawl under my blanket and not get out of bed. Other days I wanted to scream at Danica at the top of my lungs, "You are ruining your life, and you are making mine pretty awful too!" Still other days I wanted to hold Danica for hours and cradle her, as I did when she was an infant, and make the pain go away. There were days when I second-guessed everything I did as a mother and blamed myself for every possible thing that could have brought us to this place. Then there were

"Parenting by heart": giving our children the grace to fail and the strength to get back up again.

times when all I could do was go to God one more time and seek his assurance that everything was going to be all right.

I wanted to be a perfect mother; but the truth is, I did some things right, and I did some things wrong. I had to ask for forgiveness often. In the process I discovered a great deal about my humanity. I also discovered that God's mercy and Danica's heart were much bigger than my shortcomings.

Saying "I'm sorry" to our children is not a sign of weakness; rather, it shows incredible strength. And it keeps the doors of our children's hearts open to us. Danica and I managed through all the heartache and pain to remain very close to each other. We both fully understood that what we were going through wasn't easy for either of us. The victory came when we refused to blame each other and instead chose to pursue understanding, forgiveness, and reconciliation.

Allow me to share the Mom Award I received from Danica on her wedding day:

Mom,

Finally it's here. This day, this incredible event, couldn't have even fluttered through my imagination without you.

When I try to conjure up a creative way to express how thankful I am for all you've done, I can only come up with poetic clichés that are a disappointment at best. So I am going to have to ask you to simply hear what I am saying as if these words had never been used before.

You're the best, Mom. And this means so much to me. Whether or not we had a beautiful cake or exquisite flowers, thick or thin ribbon, or even a Cinderella dream dress—I still would have had a perfect day. But every little thing you did to make this day amazing, every extra dollar you spent, simply told me you loved me. Very much.

And I love you too, very much. . . .

Thank you for being who you are. I know there will be a day when I will look in the mirror and see your face, and I am so happy that I can look forward to that day. I'll be proud to be just like you.

You've given so much, and you have gone through a lot in order to be the mother I needed. I know there are many things that I would do differently if I could start again, but you never told me, "That's enough," even when my life brought you so much pain. Instead, you taught me to learn from it and to grow stronger from the hard times. You led by example, and you are still leading.

I love you, Mom. As a friend, as a mentor, as a hero. I know that we have a lot of chapters ahead of us, and there will be so many more times when I will need you to lead the way. So keep going. I'm so proud of you. And I am right behind you, cheering the whole way.

Ending this letter is proving very difficult. I've had to stop three times now to calm down and collect myself. I'm not very good at endings. New adventures are always greeted with one smile and three tears. In this case, I think I have filled a bathtub already.

I love you, Mom. And I know that when I stop crying, it's only going to get better.

Love,

Danica Joy

Oh, what joy it is to be a mother! Let's be the examples that our sons and daughters need us to be. The results will be nothing short of miraculous.

Future generations will
also serve him.
Our children will hear about
the wonders of the Lord.
His righteous acts will be
told to those yet unborn.
They will hear about
everything he has done.

—PSALM 22:30–31

The Miracle in a Mother's Faith

*I*n the last chapter, we talked about the importance of a mother's example. Perhaps in no area is this example more important than in the area of faith. Our faith in God leads to miracles—not only in our lives but also in the lives of our children. When we teach and model faith to our sons and daughters, we help ensure that heaven-sent miracles mark their lives and bless future generations. Sharing our faith is like giving a hug that lasts for all eternity. Nothing says "I love you" more.

Going to the Word

*G*od has designed a mother to be a natural mentor to her children—that is, to be the person who teaches life skills to them through encouragement and example. Yet I often meet women who feel inadequate to mentor their children because *they* were not mentored properly by their own parents. I don't think that's a valid excuse—at least not anymore. Today we have a countless number of tools available to us—books, tapes, videos, seminars—to teach us how to be the mothers and mentors God created us to be. And the best tool of all is one that has been available to mothers for hundreds of years: the Word of God. The Bible is full of wisdom about raising children, making decisions, maintaining relationships, and virtually every other topic that's important for living life well. As moms, the smartest thing we can do is go to the Scriptures regularly for wisdom. We demonstrate our faith when we show our children that we depend upon and obey God's Word.

The Bible is a very practical book. For example, Titus 2:4–5 encourages older women to "train the younger women to love their husbands and children, to live wisely and be pure, to take care of their homes, to do good, and to be submissive to their husbands." Personally, I know that so much of what I have learned about parenting (and about life in general) has come from the examples of other incredible women who have modeled particular life skills for me. The Titus 2 principle works! Whenever we find ourselves struggling in our roles as moms, we need to listen to the Bible and learn from other women who've already successfully "been there, done that." That's wisdom!

Serving Others

The Bible also teaches this principle: if we want to be great in God's kingdom, we must learn to be the servants of all. What an incredible thought! This means that *anybody* can be great, because anybody can serve.

Service is a wonderful mentoring tool, because those whom we serve, we influence. In fact, service is one of the best ways for us to positively influence others. Every gesture of kindness that finds its expression in service travels deep into the heart of the recipient and comes back to bless the giver in significant ways. This is true in families and in life in general.

As mothers, we know what it is to serve. We serve our families in many ordinary ways on a daily basis: cooking, cleaning, washing, and teaching, to name a few. When we do these things, we not only bless and influence our children; we honor God.

We transcend these ordinary acts of service, however, when we allow our hearts to reach out in creative and magnificent ways to touch the hearts of our children through special, loving acts of kindness: placing a sweet I love you note on their pillow, arranging a date for "just the two of us," reading an extra story at bedtime "just because," or offering a hug and a word of encouragement when they know a word of correction is coming. It takes so little to do something so big! But as Bobbie Houston, a precious friend and mentor in my life, says, "Kindness rules!" When we serve our children through acts of kindness that go above and beyond the ordinary, we not only show our love for them; we show our love for God.

Sharing Our Faith

God's plan is for each generation to be responsible for leading the next generation toward a personal faith in Jesus Christ. In this regard, an ounce of example is worth a ton of preaching. It is through demonstrating our faith, not just preaching it, that we perpetuate it.

The biggest "hug" my amazing mother gave me when I was growing up was the example of her unwavering faith in

God. I can't recall a single moment when she ever faltered—not one moment. That's quite remarkable, especially considering that her life was not always easy. I saw her look to God, love God, praise God, cry out to God, but never once question God. She showed me

An ounce of example is worth a ton of preaching.

her faith daily in very real and practical ways. I've always wanted to be the same kind of example to my own children and to my children's children.

A verse in one of the apostle Paul's letters to Timothy is an inspiration to me. While exhorting Timothy, his spiritual son, to stir up his faith, Paul said, "I know that you sincerely trust the Lord, for you have the faith of your mother, Eunice, and your grandmother, Lois" (2 Timothy 1:5). Whenever I read this scripture, I am reminded that as I was raising my children, I was also raising my grandchildren. Children look to their moms to see faith in action. What we show them not only impacts them; it impacts future generations.

One of my fondest memories of faith in action took place at Angela's birthday party the day she turned seven. I remember her running up to me, full of excitement, and telling me that one of her little friends had asked her about going to heaven. "Mommy, should I pray with her to ask Jesus into her heart?" she asked me.

At that time in our lives, John and I were helping our church lead the youth program, so our home was often filled to the rafters with teenagers. Our girls loved being around the older kids and would often observe us teaching them, praying with them, leading them in worship, and just playing silly games with them.

"Go ahead," I encouraged her.

I have to admit, I stood around the corner and eavesdropped on what turned out to be a most precious conversation. Angela asked her friend to bow her head, close her eyes, and "repeat after me." Then she led her friend in a prayer to accept Jesus. How wonderful it was to see my daughter do so easily what she had seen John and me do so many times before with the teens! Leading her friend to Christ was as natural to Angela as it could possibly be!

Several years later we heard that this friend of Angela's had died very suddenly, and a great sadness came over all of us. But in a moment of realization, Angela's tears turned to a smile. She told me she knew her friend was in heaven. Then she went to her room and wrote a letter to the parents of this young girl. She brought it to me and asked me to put it in the mail. The message in the letter melted my heart! It went something like this: "I know you must be very sad and have a hole in your heart, because you miss your daughter very much. But I know how you can see her again, because she is in heaven, and you can go there too. You just have to ask Jesus to come into your heart. Then when you die you will be in heaven, where she lives now." I prayed over the letter as I put it in the mailbox, confident that the faith of a child would lead these grieving parents toward a God who loves them very much.

We have to remember: our children are watching us. Are we showing them how to seek godly wisdom for their lives? Are we teaching them about God's kindness, compassion, and sacrificial love? Are they learning about the power of faith? As moms, we need to make sure that our faith is living and active and demonstrated in ways that our children can see and experience. After all, there are miracles in a mother's faith—especially when that faith is transferred into the lives of her kids.

A mother is someone who walks in front of you
When you need footsteps to follow.
Behind you when you need encouragement,
And beside you when you need a friend.

—RENEE DUVALL

The Miracle in a Mother's Friendship

The brief verse by Renee Duvall that opens this chapter is inscribed on a plaque my daughter Angela gave me on Mother's Day a number of years ago. The words have continued to inspire me in my role as a mother to my children. My daughters are fully grown now, with husbands and families of their own. But they have made it clear: I still have a place in their lives. I am still a mother, yes. But I am also a friend.

Inherent in a mother's hug is her friendship. When we show love to our children consistently over the years—when we hug them, encourage them, and commit ourselves to be there for them; when we share our faith with them and influence them in ways that bring blessing to their lives—we prepare the groundwork for a wonderful and lasting friendship.

Arrows in Our Hands

In my many years as a mother, I have come to understand that from the very moment our children enter our lives, we begin to prepare them to leave. Over much time and through many transitional stages, we work to equip them to be successful in life on their own—without us. That's our job!

The Bible tells us in Psalm 127:3–5 NASB:

> Behold, children are a gift of the LORD,
> The fruit of the womb is a reward.
> Like arrows in the hand of a warrior,
> So are the children of one's youth.
> How blessed is the man whose quiver is full of
> them;
> They will not be ashamed
> When they speak with their enemies in the gate.

I love that the Bible refers to children as arrows. An arrow is something that you hold in your hand for a little while before eventually releasing it to hit a particular target. The question is, what's the target? Personally, I have tried to aim my children toward the target of a vital and flourishing relationship with God. Through the years, my desire has been for each of them to fully understand that she is created to contribute her gifts and best efforts to a God-centered life, and that by living such a life, God himself will lead her to fulfillment in every arena—spiritually, emotionally, physically, and relationally.

Of course, knowing the target doesn't mean that it's easy to hit the target. As I've said before, extraordinary outcomes require extraordinary effort. As moms, we must commit ourselves to being tenacious warriors on our children's behalf.

Roots and Wings

Our relationships with our children go through stages, because our children go through stages as they move from infancy to adulthood. The first stage of their lives, of course, is dependency. They look to their mothers/fathers for absolutely everything. A mother's face is like a mirror to them; in her eyes they see who they are and who they can become. Eventually they move on and become more independent; they begin to be more responsible for their actions and choices. Then, finally, they cross over into interdependence, where a mutual exchange of responsibility takes place between parent and child. I observed my own children pass through each of these stages with absolute wonder, watching as they stretched and believed in themselves and eventually came to a place of confidence that they would be great women, wives, and mothers—which, in fact, they are!

In the process I discovered the two most important things we can give our children: roots and wings. Roots keep them grounded; wings help them soar. As mothers, we need the wisdom to know how and when to release our children to their fullest potential without holding them back. We need the wisdom to be both coach and friend—to be someone who supports them but also lets them go.

I discovered the two most important things we can give our children: roots and wings.

Some mothers never enjoy the beauty of friendship with their children because they refuse to give up control. Controlling mothers are insecure mothers. They use manipulation—a perversion of influence—to achieve their goals. The fact is, pure friendship cannot exist where there is no freedom. Many children deliberately move away from their parents as soon as they're old enough, simply to get away from feeling dominated and controlled. On the other hand, a mother who is secure in her role and who knows who she is doesn't feel the need to control her children; rather, she wants to release her children at the proper time to experience all that life holds for them. This kind of mother can become a true friend.

I will never forget the day I broke the news to my mother that I had fallen in love with Johnnie Burns and that he was probably going to ask me to marry him. I was all of eighteen years old at the time! She looked at me in a way that only my mother can, and her eyes pierced my very soul.

"So you think you are old enough to get married?" she said. "Then you have to understand that you are old enough to *stay* married. You have to know that when you and John get married, you will have some hard times, but you can't come home."

I swallowed hard on that comment, but I knew Mom was telling me that she believed in me. She was saying that if I was going to make a choice that would affect the rest of my life, I had better make it a good one. She empowered me to take personal responsibility for my future. I am very grateful for her words, because they gave me the motivation I needed to work through some of the rough spots John and I hit early in our marriage.

A Threefold Cord

Today I enjoy magnificent friendships with my daughters. They often accompany me on my many ministry trips, and they love to get together for lunch or to go shopping. They call me when they need advice, and I call them when I need advice. We are on the journey of life together, loving and supporting one another and cheering each other on.

We understand that we need one another. Ecclesiastes 4:9–12 NKJV presents a powerful picture of just how much:

Two are better than one,
Because they have a good reward for their labor.
For if they fall, one will lift up his companion.
But woe to him who is alone when he falls,

For he has no one to help him up.

Again, if two lie down together, they will keep warm;

But how can one be warm alone?

Though one may be overpowered by another, two
    can withstand him.

And a threefold cord is not quickly broken.

Each of us was created by God to live life interdependently
with others. Our purpose cannot be fulfilled in isolation! That's
why friendship with our children has such beauty and power.
We need the friendship of the ones we love most in life in order
to be the strong, secure, successful women God created us to be.

I want to end this chapter with another treasure from my
treasure chest—my Mom Award from my youngest daughter,
Ashley (who is pregnant with her first child as I write). I love
how she expresses her longing to stay friends for life:

Dear Mom,

*You are an incredible woman. Everything that you have
done for me is so amazing. I feel so blessed to be a part of
our family. All the people I know don't have what we have*

and wish they did, and it's all because my mother loves me so much. Never for one moment have I doubted it—ever!

I want to thank you so much for all you have done to make my wedding as special as it was. It was what I have dreamt about since I was a little girl. I know life will be wonderful from now on, but I can't help but feel sad because I will be missing life with you at home. I know that we work together, but that's not good enough. I want lots of dates, because you know I can't live without one of my best friends.

You mean the world to me, and I want my life to be a tribute to your and Dad's strength.

I love you,
Ashley

I want to leave a legacy—
how will they remember me?
Did I choose to love?
Did I point to you enough
to make a mark on things—
I want to leave an offering—
A child of mercy and grace
who blessed your name unapologetically
And leave that kind of legacy.

—NICHOLE NORDEMAN

Watch for Miracles!

Several years ago I had an epiphany that put the message of this book into perspective for me. I was ministering at the exceptional Hillsong Church in Sydney, Australia. That particular morning I was teaching a group of about 450 Bible college students who had gathered from the four corners of the world. What a great honor God had given me! As I stood on the platform of that amazing church—one that is impacting the world in many ways—I realized that I had not gotten there on my own. I had been carried there.

At that moment, I felt an overpowering sense of my grandmother's presence in my life. I realized that her love, her prayers, and her belief in me were huge factors in forming the woman I had become—the woman who was now speaking to hundreds of hungry Bible students in a most amazing setting.

My beloved Oma, who spoke in broken English, lived a very simple, difficult, but influential, life. Five of her eleven children died at early ages; she experienced deep personal tragedy. With my grandfather, she fled Russia when she was pregnant with her first child, never to see her parents again. She and my grandfather arrived in Paraguay, South America, as refugees and began their new life in the dry, hot, barren Chaco Desert. The circumstances were dire and life was hard, but Oma's heart never hardened. Instead, she raised her children to love God passionately, instilling a vital faith within each one of them.

I must be one of God's favorites, I thought, *because I was honored to have this amazing woman as my Oma and blessed to be raised by her daughter, my mother, Elsy.* I knew that my being in that place at that moment was a miracle—a miracle produced by a mother's hug, a grandmother's hug, and all of the love and support that those hugs encompassed.

A Living Legend

*O*ma is in heaven today, but my mother is very much here on earth, still being her amazing self. As impacted as I was by my grandmother, no one has shaped my life more than my mother. I fully understand the miracle in a mommy's hug, because I have lived my entire life in the warmth and security of it.

My mother has influenced me in ways that will carry me through the remainder of my life. To me she is a living legend. I will forever remember my mother's stubborn tenacity to fight for what is right; her infectious laughter; her big, beautiful heart; her dedication and love for my father (and her endless flirtations with him); her kindness (I could bring stray cats and a carload of friends home whenever I wanted to); her bountiful table that was always set for a few extra guests; her prayers that would never let me go; her consistent encouragement (she believes I can do anything!); her exemplary character, which she still demonstrates daily toward me, my family, and the people in our world—I could go on and on.

As I write this, tears are flowing, because I feel so blessed. My mother set me up to win in life. She sacrificially created an environment for me to flourish in, and her godly influence parented me well. I have endeavored to pass on her legacy through my own children and through my children's children. The story continues to be written. I believe it will have a great ending.

Miracles in the Making

Children, after all, are like seeds growing in soil that we help prepare for them. They flourish best in an atmosphere of loving care—in homes where hugs from Mom are plentiful, love is unconditional, and the soil is full of nutrients derived from a mother's touch, her presence, her encouragement, her influence, her commitment, her example, her faith, and ultimately, her friendship.

In the introduction to this book, I quoted something that John wrote in *The Miracle in a Daddy's Hug*. I want to paraphrase him now as we close:

A mother's hug is simple and portable. It's weightless and

convenient. It's powerful, durable, limitless, expandable, applicable, enjoyable, and free. And best of all, it works! So go ahead, wrap your arms around your child. Don't hold back. Don't ever stop. Hug and keep on hugging.

And watch for a miracle.[1]

notes

introduction: *The Miracle in a Mother's Hug*

1. John Burns, *The Miracle in a Daddy's Hug* (West Monroe, La.: Howard Publishing, 2003), xii–xiii.

2. Ibid., xiii.

chapter two: *The Miracle in a Mother's Presence*

1. Harry Chapin, "The Cat's in the Cradle," *Harry Chapin: Story of a Life* (Rhino Records, 1999). Permission pending.

chapter five: *The Miracle in a Mother's Commitment*

1. Dialogue from *Fiddler on the Roof* (MGM/United Artists, 1971). Produced and directed by Norman Jewison; screenplay by Joseph Stein. Based on the book *Tevye's Daughters* by Sholom Aleichem.

epilogue: *Watch for Miracles!*

Epigraph. Nichole Nordeman, "Legacy," *Woven and Spun* (Sparrow Records, 2002). Used by permission.

1. Burns, *The Miracle in a Daddy's Hug*, 91.

There's a
Miracle in a
Daddy's Hug too!

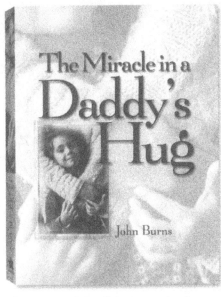

The perfect companion to *The Miracle in a Mother's Hug* was written by Helen Burn's husband, John. In his book you will learn of Helen and John's struggle with the eating disorder of their middle daughter and the miraculous effects of his tender hug.

Chapter titles include:

The Miracle in a Child
The Miracle in a Daddy's Words
The Miracle in a Daddy's Time
The Miracle in a Daddy's Love
The Miracle in a Daddy's Faith

John Burns, cohost of the international program *Family Success,* understands the complex issues our children face and in this book shares a message of hope, healing, and unconditional love. Fathers who learn how to express their love to their children will discover that the miracle in their hugs blesses not only their children but themselves as well.

THE **M♥therhood** CLUB

Making a Difference One Kiss at a Time

mc

...born from a simple idea: *honor Mom for doing the most important job in the world.*

Titles included in THE **M♥therhood** CLUB:

Prayer Guide: *The Busy Mom's Guide to Prayer*
—Lisa Whelchel

Parenting: *Mom-PhD*
—Teresa Bell Kindred

There's a Perfect Little Angel in Every Child
—Gigi Schweikert

Inspiration: *The Miracle in a Mother's Hug*
—Helen Burns

Gift: *Holding the World by the Hand*
—Gigi Schweikert

Fiction: *Tight Squeeze*
—Debbie DiGiovanni

Devotional: *"I'm a Good Mother"*
—Gigi Schweikert

"At The Motherhood Club, you'll find books to meet all your mothering needs."
—Lisa Whelchel
(From The Facts of Life)

Printed in the United States
By Bookmasters